MASTERING

THE RSI INDICATOR

by

Lalit Mohanty

Table of Contents:

- Real-world examples and case studies

Chapter 5: Overbought and Oversold Conditions

- Understanding overbought and oversold signals

- Trading strategies for overbought and oversold markets

- Common misconceptions and pitfalls

Chapter 6: RSI Trend Analysis

- Integrating RSI into trend analysis

- Using RSI to confirm or challenge trend directions

- Strategies for trend-following and trend-reversal scenarios

Chapter 7: Combining RSI with Other Indicators

- Enhancing trading signals with multiple indicators

- Common indicator pairings and their synergies

- Avoiding redundancy and conflicting signals

Chapter 8: RSI in Different Markets

- Adapting RSI to various financial instruments

- Stocks, Forex, commodities, and cryptocurrencies

- Market-specific considerations and nuances

Chapter 9: RSI Trading Strategies

- **Building effective trading strategies around RSI**

- **Short-term and long-term approaches**

- **Backtesting and optimizing RSI-based strategies**

Chapter 10: RSI and Risk Management

- **Managing risk with RSI signals**

- **Position sizing based on RSI analysis**

- **Setting stop-loss and take-profit levels**

Chapter 11: Psychological Aspects of RSI Trading

- **Emotions and discipline in RSI-based trading**

- **Common psychological challenges and how to overcome them**

- **Maintaining a balanced mindset during market fluctuations**

Chapter 12: Case Studies

- **Detailed analysis of successful RSI trades**

- **Learning from mistakes and losses**

- **Real-world applications of RSI in diverse market scenarios**

Chapter 13: RSI and Market Sentiment

PREFACE

This book aims to equip traders with a deep understanding of the RSI indicator and the skills necessary to apply it effectively in their trading strategies. Through a combination of theory, practical examples, and real-life case studies, readers will gain the expertise needed to master the RSI indicator and enhance their overall trading success.

CHAPTER 1

INTRODUCTION TO RSI

The Relative Strength Index, or RSI, stands as a cornerstone in the realm of technical analysis, offering traders a powerful tool to gauge the strength and momentum of price movements. In this introductory chapter, we will delve into the fundamental aspects of the RSI, tracing its historical origins, understanding its calculation, and emphasizing its significance in technical analysis.

Understanding the Basics of the Relative Strength Index

At its core, the Relative Strength Index is a momentum oscillator that measures the speed and change of price movements. Developed by J. Welles Wilder and introduced to the public in his 1978 book, "New Concepts in Technical Trading Systems," the RSI quickly gained popularity for its ability to identify overbought or oversold conditions in a market.

The RSI is typically calculated using the average gain and average loss over a specified period, which is usually 14 periods. The resulting index, expressed on a scale from 0 to 100, provides traders with a visual representation of the strength of a security's recent price movements.

Interpreting RSI values involves assessing whether an asset is potentially overbought (RSI above 70), suggesting it may be due for a price correction, or oversold (RSI below 30), indicating a potential buying opportunity. However, the true power of the RSI lies in its versatility, extending beyond mere overbought and oversold indications to encompass trend analysis, divergence patterns, and more.

Historical Background and Development of RSI

To appreciate the RSI fully, it is essential to delve into its historical roots. J. Welles Wilder, a prolific technical analyst, introduced the RSI as part of a broader effort to enhance the toolkit available to traders. Wilder's goal was to create an indicator that could not only identify the strength of price movements but also help traders navigate the intricacies of market trends.

The RSI was revolutionary for its time, providing a quantitative measure of the strength of price changes rather than relying solely on visual analysis. Its introduction marked a paradigm shift in technical analysis, offering a systematic approach to understanding market momentum.

Significance of RSI in Technical Analysis

In the vast landscape of technical analysis, the RSI occupies a unique position as a momentum indicator. Traders and analysts worldwide use it to make informed decisions about when to enter or exit positions, helping to optimize risk and reward. The RSI's ability to identify potential trend reversals, confirm existing trends, and signal overextended conditions makes it an invaluable tool in the trader's arsenal.

As we progress through this book, we will explore the intricacies of the RSI, unraveling its various applications in different market conditions, and providing you with the knowledge and skills needed to harness its full potential. Whether you are a novice trader or a seasoned professional, mastering the Relative Strength Index can significantly enhance your ability to navigate the complexities of financial markets.

CHAPTER 2

CALCULATING RSI

Understanding the Relative Strength Index (RSI) requires a clear comprehension of its calculation process. In this chapter, we will provide a step-by-step guide to RSI calculation, elucidate the underlying formula, and guide you through the interpretation of RSI values.

Step-by-Step Guide to RSI Calculation

1. **Select a Time Period:** The first step in calculating RSI is choosing a time period, often referred to as "N," which is typically set to 14 periods. This means that RSI will be calculated based on the average gains and losses over the last 14 price bars or periods.

2. **Calculate Average Gain and Average Loss:**

- Calculate the daily price changes (gains or losses) over the selected period.

- Separate the gains and losses into two groups.

- Calculate the average gain and average loss separately.

3. **Calculate Relative Strength (RS):**

- Divide the average gain by the average loss to obtain the relative strength (RS).

RS = Average gain / average loss

Calculate RSI:

- Use the following formula to calculate the RSI:

RSI = 100-(100/1+RS)

Explaining the Formula and Its Components

- **Average Gain and Average Loss:**

  - The average gain is the average of all positive price changes over the selected period.

  - The average loss is the average of all negative price changes over the selected period.

- **Relative Strength (RS):**

- RS measures the ratio of average gain to average loss.

- A higher RS indicates stronger upward price momentum, while a lower RS suggests stronger downward momentum.

- **RSI Formula:**

  - RSI is calculated using a scale of 0 to 100.

  - RSI values above 70 are considered overbought, suggesting a potential reversal or correction.

  - RSI values below 30 are considered oversold, indicating a potential buying opportunity.

  - The formula compresses the RS into a scale that oscillates between 0 and 100, making it easier for traders to interpret and compare across different securities and timeframes.

Interpreting RSI Values

- **Overbought Conditions (RSI > 70):**

  - RSI values above 70 suggest that the asset may be overbought.

  - Traders often interpret this as a signal to sell or take profits, anticipating a potential price correction.

- **Oversold Conditions (RSI < 30):**

- RSI values below 30 suggest that the asset may be oversold.

- Traders may see this as a potential buying opportunity, anticipating a price rebound.

- **Neutral Zone (RSI between 30 and 70):**

  - RSI values between 30 and 70 are often considered neutral.

  - Traders may use other indicators or tools to complement RSI signals in this range.

Understanding the intricacies of RSI calculation and interpretation is essential for effectively incorporating this powerful indicator into your trading strategy. In the subsequent chapters, we will explore various applications and strategies to harness the full potential of RSI in different market conditions.

CHAPTER 3

RSI PARAMETERS AND SETTINGS

The Relative Strength Index (RSI) is a versatile tool, and its effectiveness can be greatly influenced by the choice of parameters and settings. In this chapter, we will delve into the critical aspects of selecting the right period for RSI, fine-tuning sensitivity across various timeframes, and customizing RSI settings to align with specific market conditions.

Choosing the Right Period for RSI

The RSI's default period is 14, as proposed by its creator, J. Welles Wilder. This means that the indicator considers the average gains and losses over the past 14 periods. While this setting is widely used and accepted, it's essential to recognize that different timeframes may warrant different RSI periods.

- **Short-Term Trading (Intraday):**

  - Traders engaging in intraday trading might opt for shorter RSI periods, such as 9 or 10, to capture more immediate price movements.

  - Shorter periods can provide quicker signals but may also be more prone to noise.

- **Medium-Term Trading (Daily to Weekly):**

  - For swing traders or those focusing on daily to weekly charts, the default 14-period RSI may suffice.

  - This setting offers a balanced view of short-term and medium-term price trends.

- **Long-Term Investing (Monthly):**

  - Investors with a long-term perspective may use longer RSI periods, such as 21 or 28, to filter out short-term fluctuations and emphasize broader trends.

Selecting the appropriate period is a crucial decision influenced by your trading or investment horizon and risk tolerance.

Fine-Tuning Sensitivity with Different Timeframes

The sensitivity of the RSI can be adjusted by modifying the timeframe. This involves selecting the appropriate number of periods for analysis. Here are some considerations:

- **Increasing Sensitivity:**

    - Shorter timeframes and lower RSI periods increase sensitivity, generating more frequent signals.

    - This can be advantageous in fast-moving markets but may lead to more false signals.

- **Decreasing Sensitivity:**

    - Longer timeframes and higher RSI periods reduce sensitivity, filtering out noise and providing more reliable signals.

    - This approach is suitable for smoother, trending markets but may result in delayed signals.

Understanding the trade-off between sensitivity and reliability is pivotal for optimizing RSI performance.

Customizing RSI Settings for Specific Market Conditions

Markets are dynamic, and RSI settings should adapt to prevailing conditions. Customizing RSI settings involves adjusting parameters based on the characteristics of the asset or market being analyzed.

- **Volatility Considerations:**

- In highly volatile markets, using a longer RSI period may help smooth out fluctuations.

- Conversely, in low-volatility environments, a shorter RSI period may be more responsive to subtle changes.

- **Trend Strength:**

  - Assess the strength of the prevailing trend before choosing RSI settings.

  - In strong trending markets, a longer RSI period may be appropriate, while in sideways markets, a shorter period may yield more relevant signals.

- **Combining RSI with Other Indicators:**

  - RSI is often more effective when used in conjunction with other indicators.

  - Experiment with combining RSI with moving averages, trendlines, or other oscillators to enhance your analysis.

By customizing RSI settings based on market conditions and your trading preferences, you can fine-tune this powerful indicator to align more closely with your strategic goals. In the subsequent chapters, we will explore advanced RSI techniques and strategies, building upon the foundation laid in this chapter.

CHAPTER 4

BULLISH AND BEARISH DIVERGENCE

Divergence patterns are integral to the predictive power of the Relative Strength Index (RSI). In this chapter, we'll explore the identification of divergence patterns with RSI, delve into the interpretation of bullish and bearish divergence, and elucidate these concepts through real-world examples and case studies.

Identifying Divergence Patterns with RSI

Divergence occurs when the price of an asset moves in a direction opposite to that of the RSI. There are two main types of divergence: bullish and bearish.

- **Bullish Divergence:**

- Occurs when the price makes a lower low, but the RSI forms a higher low.

- Suggests that while prices are declining, the momentum behind the decline is weakening, indicating a potential reversal to the upside.

- **Bearish Divergence:**

  - Occurs when the price makes a higher high, but the RSI forms a lower high.

  - Suggests that while prices are rising, the momentum behind the ascent is weakening, signaling a potential reversal to the downside.

Identifying divergence patterns can provide traders with early warnings of potential trend reversals, offering valuable insights into the underlying market dynamics.

How to Interpret and Trade Bullish and Bearish Divergence

Interpreting divergence involves understanding the underlying dynamics between price and momentum. Here's a step-by-step guide:

- **Bullish Divergence Interpretation:**

  1. Identify a lower low in the price chart.

  2. Simultaneously, observe a higher low forming on the RSI.

3. This suggests that although prices are declining, the momentum behind the decline is diminishing.

4. Consider this a potential signal that a bullish reversal may be imminent.

- **Bearish Divergence Interpretation:**

    1. Identify a higher high in the price chart.

    2. Simultaneously, observe a lower high forming on the RSI.

    3. This indicates that, despite rising prices, the momentum behind the ascent is waning.

    4. View this as a potential signal that a bearish reversal may be on the horizon.

Real-World Examples and Case Studies

Let's examine a real-world example of bullish divergence:

- **Example: Bullish Divergence**

    - **Price Action:** A stock exhibits a series of lower lows, indicating a downtrend.

    - **RSI Action:** Concurrently, the RSI forms higher lows, signaling a weakening downside momentum.

- **Trade Decision:** Traders might interpret this as a potential bullish reversal signal and consider entering a long position.

Now, consider a case of bearish divergence:

- **Example: Bearish Divergence**

  - **Price Action:** An asset shows a sequence of higher highs, signaling an uptrend.

  - **RSI Action:** Simultaneously, the RSI forms lower highs, suggesting a diminishing upside momentum.

  - **Trade Decision:** Traders might interpret this as a potential bearish reversal signal and consider entering a short position.

Through these examples, it becomes evident that divergence patterns on the RSI can serve as powerful precursors to trend reversals, enabling traders to anticipate market shifts and make informed decisions.

As we progress through this guide, we'll continue to explore various applications of RSI, building a comprehensive understanding of its capabilities in diverse market scenarios.

CHAPTER 5

OVERBOUGHT AND OVERSOLD CONDITIONS

The concepts of overbought and oversold conditions lie at the heart of Relative Strength Index (RSI) analysis. In this chapter, we will delve into the understanding of overbought and oversold signals, explore trading strategies tailored for these market conditions, and address common misconceptions and pitfalls associated with interpreting RSI extremes.

Understanding Overbought and Oversold Signals

The RSI oscillates between 0 and 100, with traditional thresholds marking overbought conditions when RSI is above 70 and oversold conditions when RSI is below 30.

These levels indicate potential exhaustion in the prevailing trend.

- **Overbought Conditions (RSI > 70):**
  - Suggests that the asset may have experienced a substantial price increase, and there's a possibility of a price correction.
  - Traders might interpret this as a signal to consider selling or taking profits.

- **Oversold Conditions (RSI < 30):**
  - Indicates that the asset may have undergone a significant price decrease, and there's a potential for a price rebound.
  - Traders might interpret this as a signal to consider buying or entering a long position.

Understanding these signals provides a basis for implementing various trading strategies based on RSI extremes.

Trading Strategies for Overbought and Oversold Markets

1. **Overbought Market Strategies:**
   - **Bearish Divergence Confirmation:** Look for bearish divergence as confirmation when RSI is in overbought territory. If the price is making

new highs, but RSI is making lower highs, it may signal a potential trend reversal to the downside.

- **Overbought Reversal:** When RSI moves above 70, consider selling or shorting the asset, anticipating a potential pullback.

2. **Oversold Market Strategies:**

- **Bullish Divergence Confirmation:** Look for bullish divergence when RSI is in oversold territory. If the price is making new lows, but RSI is making higher lows, it may signal a potential trend reversal to the upside.

- **Oversold Reversal:** When RSI drops below 30, consider buying or entering a long position, anticipating a potential bounce or reversal.

Common Misconceptions and Pitfalls

1. **Continuous Overbought or Oversold Conditions:**

- A common misconception is assuming that an asset will immediately reverse when it enters overbought or oversold conditions. RSI extremes can persist during strong trends, and an overbought market can become even more overbought before a reversal occurs.

2. **Ignoring Price Action:**

- RSI should be used in conjunction with price action and other indicators. Overbought or oversold conditions are more reliable when they align with other technical signals or chart patterns.

3. **Using RSI in Isolation:**

- RSI works best when used as part of a comprehensive trading strategy. Relying solely on RSI without considering other factors may lead to suboptimal decisions.

4. **Static RSI Settings:**

- Markets evolve, and using static RSI settings for all assets and timeframes may not be optimal. Adjust RSI settings based on market conditions, volatility, and the specific characteristics of the asset being analyzed.

By understanding the nuances of overbought and oversold conditions, implementing effective trading strategies, and being aware of common misconceptions, traders can leverage the power of RSI to make informed decisions in dynamic market environments. As we progress, we'll explore more advanced RSI techniques and their applications.

CHAPTER 6

RSI TREND ANALYSIS

The Relative Strength Index (RSI) is not limited to identifying overbought or oversold conditions; it is also a potent tool for trend analysis. In this chapter, we will explore the integration of RSI into trend analysis, understand how to use RSI to confirm or challenge trend directions, and uncover strategies for both trend-following and trend-reversal scenarios.

Integrating RSI into Trend Analysis

Traditionally, traders use moving averages, trendlines, and other trend indicators to assess the direction of a market trend. RSI, when incorporated into trend analysis, adds a dynamic layer by measuring the momentum behind price movements.

- **Trend Confirmation with RSI:**

  - During an uptrend, RSI tends to stay in the upper range (above 50), reflecting strong upward momentum.

  - In a downtrend, RSI generally stays in the lower range (below 50), indicating robust downward momentum.

- **Potential Trend Reversal Signals:**

  - Divergence between RSI and price action can serve as an early warning for a potential trend reversal.

  - Bullish divergence in a downtrend or bearish divergence in an uptrend may signal a weakening trend.

Using RSI to Confirm or Challenge Trend Directions

1. **Confirming an Uptrend with RSI:**

   - In a strong uptrend, RSI typically remains in the upper range (above 50).

   - Look for RSI to consistently make higher highs and higher lows, aligning with the upward price movement.

2. **Confirming a Downtrend with RSI:**

- In a robust downtrend, RSI tends to stay in the lower range (below 50).

- Observe RSI making lower highs and lower lows, in sync with the downward price movement.

3. **Challenging the Trend with Divergence:**

- Bullish Divergence: In a downtrend, if RSI forms higher lows while prices make lower lows, it may signal a weakening downtrend and potential reversal.

- Bearish Divergence: In an uptrend, if RSI forms lower highs while prices make higher highs, it may indicate a weakening uptrend and potential reversal.

Strategies for Trend-Following and Trend-Reversal Scenarios

1. **Trend-Following with RSI:**

- **Overbought/Oversold Confirmation:** In a strong uptrend, look for buying opportunities when RSI pulls back to oversold levels but remains above 50. In a downtrend, consider selling when RSI rallies to overbought levels but stays below 50.

- **Trendline Support/Resistance:** Use RSI to confirm support or resistance at trendlines. In an uptrend, a bounce off trendline support with RSI confirmation can be a strong entry signal.

2. **Trend-Reversal with RSI:**

- **Divergence Confirmation:** Combine divergence signals with other reversal indicators. For example, look for a bullish divergence near a key support level for a potential trend reversal to the upside.

- **RSI Crosses 50:** In a potential trend reversal, watch for RSI crossing the 50 level. Crossing from below to above 50 may signal a shift from a downtrend to an uptrend, and vice versa.

By seamlessly integrating RSI into trend analysis and understanding its role in both confirming and challenging trend directions, traders can enhance their ability to make well-informed decisions in various market scenarios. As we progress, we will explore more advanced RSI techniques and their applications in different trading strategies.

CHAPTER 7

COMBINING RSI WITH OTHER INDICATORS

Effective trading often involves a comprehensive approach, and combining the Relative Strength Index (RSI) with other indicators can significantly enhance the quality of trading signals. In this chapter, we will explore the benefits of integrating RSI with other indicators, examine common pairings and their synergies, and discuss strategies for avoiding redundancy and conflicting signals.

Enhancing Trading Signals with Multiple Indicators

The combination of RSI with other indicators creates a more robust analytical framework, allowing traders to filter out noise and generate more accurate signals. Each indicator provides unique insights into different aspects of price action and market dynamics.

- **Confirmation of Trend:**

  - Combining RSI with trend-following indicators such as Moving Averages or trendlines helps confirm the prevailing trend.

  - For example, in an uptrend, RSI above 50 combined with a rising Moving Average strengthens the bullish case.

- **Volume Analysis:**

  - Incorporating volume indicators, like On-Balance Volume (OBV) or volume-based moving averages, alongside RSI can provide additional confirmation or divergence signals.

  - Rising prices with increasing volume can enhance the strength of a bullish trend, while decreasing volume in a downtrend might suggest weakening bearish momentum.

- **Volatility Measures:**

  - Combining RSI with volatility indicators, such as Bollinger Bands, can help identify potential breakouts or breakdowns.

- High RSI values in conjunction with the upper Bollinger Band may indicate overextension, potentially preceding a reversal.

Common Indicator Pairings and Their Synergies

1. **Moving Averages and RSI:**

   - **Synergy:** Moving Averages help smooth price trends, providing a clear picture of the overall direction. Combining Moving Averages with RSI can confirm trends and identify potential reversals.

   - **Example:** Confirming a bullish trend with RSI above 50 and prices trading above a rising 50-day Moving Average.

2. **MACD (Moving Average Convergence Divergence) and RSI:**

   - **Synergy:** MACD is a trend-following momentum indicator. Combining MACD with RSI can offer a dual confirmation of trends and divergence signals.

   - **Example:** A bullish crossover on MACD aligning with RSI moving above 50 may strengthen a buy signal.

3. **Bollinger Bands and RSI:**

- **Synergy:** Bollinger Bands indicate volatility and potential reversal points. Combining Bollinger Bands with RSI can identify overbought or oversold conditions within the bands.

- **Example:** Prices touching the upper Bollinger Band while RSI is above 70 may indicate potential overextension and a possible reversal.

Avoiding Redundancy and Conflicting Signals

While combining indicators can provide richer insights, it's crucial to avoid redundancy and conflicting signals. Here are strategies to maintain clarity:

1. **Focus on Key Signals:**

   - Identify specific signals from each indicator that are crucial to your strategy. For example, RSI crossing 70 may be a key signal, while the Moving Average confirms the overall trend.

2. **Use Complementary Indicators:**

   - Choose indicators that complement rather than duplicate each other. Combining trend-following and momentum indicators often offers a synergistic effect.

3. **Consider Timeframes:**

- Ensure that the timeframes of the indicators align. Short-term indicators may offer different signals than long-term indicators.

4. **Monitor for Confirmation:**

   - Wait for confirmation from multiple indicators before making trading decisions. A divergence signal on RSI may be stronger if it aligns with a trend confirmation from Moving Averages.

By thoughtfully combining RSI with other indicators, traders can refine their analysis and make more informed decisions. However, it's essential to maintain a balance and avoid overwhelming the analysis with too many indicators. In the subsequent chapters, we will explore advanced RSI techniques and their applications in various trading scenarios.

CHAPTER 8

RSI IN DIFFERENT MARKETS

The adaptability of the Relative Strength Index (RSI) makes it a versatile tool applicable to various financial instruments and markets. In this chapter, we will explore the nuances of using RSI in stocks, Forex, commodities, and cryptocurrencies, addressing market-specific considerations and providing insights into optimizing RSI for diverse trading environments.

Adapting RSI to Various Financial Instruments

Different financial instruments exhibit distinct characteristics, and RSI can be adapted to suit the nuances of each market. Understanding these adaptations enhances the effectiveness of RSI analysis.

- **Stocks:**

- **Consideration:** Stocks often respond to company-specific news, earnings reports, and other events that can influence price movements.

- **Adaptation:** Incorporate fundamental analysis alongside RSI for a comprehensive view. Earnings releases or major corporate events may coincide with RSI signals.

- **Forex (Foreign Exchange):**

  - **Consideration:** Forex markets are influenced by economic indicators, geopolitical events, and interest rate differentials.

  - **Adaptation:** Monitor economic calendars and major news releases when trading Forex with RSI. Be aware of potential currency interventions and central bank actions.

- **Commodities:**

  - **Consideration:** Commodity prices are impacted by supply and demand dynamics, geopolitical factors, and weather conditions.

  - **Adaptation:** RSI signals in commodity markets can be influenced by seasonal patterns. Additionally, consider correlations with currencies and global economic conditions.

- **Cryptocurrencies:**

- **Consideration:** Cryptocurrencies are known for their high volatility and sensitivity to market sentiment.

- **Adaptation:** Cryptocurrencies may experience rapid price movements. Shorter RSI periods or combining RSI with volatility indicators can be effective. Be cautious of market sentiment and regulatory developments.

Market-Specific Considerations and Nuances

1. **Liquidity Concerns:**

   - **Stocks:** High-liquidity stocks often provide more reliable RSI signals.

   - **Cryptocurrencies:** Some smaller cryptocurrencies may experience low liquidity, leading to sharper price movements. Exercise caution and verify RSI signals with other indicators.

2. **News and Events:**

   - **Forex:** Economic data releases, interest rate decisions, and geopolitical events can significantly impact Forex markets. Stay informed about scheduled news events.

3. **Seasonal Influences:**

- **Commodities:** Agricultural commodities are often affected by seasonal factors. Adjust RSI settings or consider additional analysis during planting and harvest seasons.

4. **Global Economic Conditions:**

    - **Stocks:** Economic indicators and global economic conditions influence stock markets. RSI signals should be considered within the broader economic context.

5. **Market Sentiment:**

    - **Cryptocurrencies:** Sentiment can be a powerful driver. Monitor social media, forums, and news for shifts in sentiment that may precede price movements.

Tailoring RSI Strategies for Specific Markets

1. **Adjust Timeframes:**

    - Different markets may respond to different RSI timeframes. Experiment with varying periods to find what works best for a particular instrument.

2. **Combine with Market-Specific Indicators:**

    - Complement RSI with indicators relevant to the specific market. For example, combine RSI with commodity-specific indicators when trading commodities.

3. **Risk Management:**

   - Adapt risk management strategies based on the volatility and characteristics of the market. Cryptocurrencies, for instance, may require tighter risk controls due to their volatility.

By recognizing the unique features of each market, traders can optimize their use of RSI and develop strategies that align with the dynamics of stocks, Forex, commodities, or cryptocurrencies. As we progress, we'll delve into more advanced applications of RSI and explore its role in algorithmic trading and quantitative strategies.

CHAPTER 9

RSI TRADING STRATEGIES

Crafting effective trading strategies around the Relative Strength Index (RSI) requires a deep understanding of its dynamics and a thoughtful approach to market conditions. In this chapter, we will explore the construction of trading strategies, considering both short-term and long-term approaches, and delve into the crucial aspects of backtesting and optimizing RSI-based strategies for robust performance.

Building Effective Trading Strategies Around RSI

1. **Trend-Following Strategies:**

   - **Objective:** Capture trends and ride momentum in the direction of the prevailing market trend.

   - **Approach:**

- In an uptrend, look for RSI to remain above 50 as confirmation.

- Consider buying when RSI is oversold (below 30) in an uptrend, indicating a potential buying opportunity.

2. **Reversal Strategies:**

- **Objective:** Identify potential trend reversals before they become evident through price action.

- **Approach:**

  - Look for divergence signals between RSI and price action.

  - Consider selling when RSI is overbought (above 70) in a downtrend, signaling a potential reversal to the downside.

3. **Mean Reversion Strategies:**

- **Objective:** Exploit overbought or oversold conditions with an expectation of a return to average market conditions.

- **Approach:**

  - Buy when RSI is oversold and sell when RSI is overbought, anticipating a reversion to the mean.

4. **Combining RSI with Other Indicators:**

- **Objective:** Strengthen signals by incorporating additional technical indicators.

- **Approach:**

  - Combine RSI with Moving Averages, MACD, or Bollinger Bands to confirm signals and reduce false positives.

5. **Divergence-Based Strategies:**

- **Objective:** Identify potential reversals based on divergence patterns between RSI and price action.

- **Approach:**

  - Look for divergence signals and use them as a basis for entering or exiting trades.

Short-Term and Long-Term Approaches

1. **Short-Term Trading:**

- **Characteristics:** Intraday or swing trading with a focus on capturing short-term price movements.

- **Strategy:** Utilize shorter RSI periods (e.g., 9 or 14) for faster signals. Overbought or oversold conditions may have shorter durations.

2. **Long-Term Investing:**

   - **Characteristics:** Position trading or long-term investing with a focus on macro trends.

   - **Strategy:** Use longer RSI periods (e.g., 21 or 28) for trend confirmation. Overbought or oversold conditions may have more prolonged implications.

Backtesting and Optimizing RSI-Based Strategies

1. **Collect Historical Data:**

   - Gather historical price and indicator data for the chosen time period.

2. **Define Strategy Rules:**

   - Clearly outline the entry and exit rules based on RSI signals and other criteria.

3. **Implement Backtesting:**

   - Apply the defined rules to historical data to simulate how the strategy would have performed in the past.

4. **Evaluate Results:**

   - Analyze the performance metrics, including profitability, drawdowns, and risk-adjusted returns.

5. **Optimize Parameters:**

   - Adjust RSI periods, overbought/oversold levels, or other parameters to enhance performance based on historical data.

6. **Forward Testing:**

   - Implement the optimized strategy on more recent data to validate its effectiveness in real-time market conditions.

7. **Risk Management:**

   - Implement robust risk management techniques to protect against adverse market conditions and unexpected events.

Considerations for Successful RSI Trading Strategies:

1. **Adapt to Market Conditions:**

   - Modify strategies based on the prevailing market environment, considering volatility and trend strength.

2. **Avoid Over-Optimization:**

   - While optimization is crucial, be cautious not to over-optimize the strategy to fit historical data, which may lead to poor performance in real-world conditions.

3. **Stay Informed:**

- Monitor economic events, news, and changes in market sentiment, as external factors can impact the effectiveness of RSI signals.

4. **Continuous Improvement:**

- Regularly review and refine strategies based on ongoing market conditions and feedback from the application of the strategy.

Constructing effective RSI trading strategies requires a balance between historical analysis, adaptability to market conditions, and a commitment to continuous improvement. As we progress, we will delve into advanced RSI techniques and explore its role in algorithmic trading and quantitative strategies.

CHAPTER 10

RSI AND RISK MANAGEMENT

Risk management is a critical component of successful trading, and the Relative Strength Index (RSI) can play a pivotal role in guiding risk management decisions. In this chapter, we will explore how to manage risk using RSI signals, discuss position sizing strategies based on RSI analysis, and delve into the setting of stop-loss and take-profit levels to safeguard trading capital.

Managing Risk with RSI Signals

1. **Identifying Risk Points:**

   - Use RSI signals to identify potential risk points in the market.

   - Overbought or oversold conditions can highlight areas where the market might be prone to reversals.

2. **Confirmation with Other Indicators:**

   - Confirm RSI signals with other technical indicators to strengthen the reliability of risk assessments.

   - Combining RSI with trendlines, Moving Averages, or other oscillators can enhance risk analysis.

3. **Volatility Considerations:**

   - Factor in market volatility when interpreting RSI signals. High volatility may lead to rapid price movements, impacting risk levels.

Position Sizing Based on RSI Analysis

1. **Determine Trade Size:**

   - Adjust the size of the position based on the strength of the RSI signal and the level of conviction in the trade.

   - A strong overbought or oversold signal may warrant a larger position size.

2. **Consider Volatility:**

   - Account for market volatility when determining position size. Higher volatility may require smaller positions to accommodate larger price swings.

3. **Align Position Size with Risk Tolerance:**

- Ensure that the position size aligns with the trader's risk tolerance and overall risk management strategy.

- Avoid overcommitting capital to a single trade based solely on RSI signals.

Setting Stop-Loss and Take-Profit Levels

1. **Stop-Loss Placement:**

- **Based on RSI Levels:** Place stop-loss orders based on RSI levels. For example, if selling in an overbought condition, set a stop-loss just above the overbought level.

- **Using Price Action:** Combine RSI signals with price action to place stops above or below key support or resistance levels.

2. **Take-Profit Placement:**

- **Based on RSI Levels:** Set take-profit orders based on RSI levels. For instance, in a long position, consider taking profits when RSI enters overbought territory.

- **Using Price Targets:** Align take-profit levels with key price targets or levels identified through technical analysis.

3. **Trailing Stops:**

- Implement trailing stops that adjust with price movements and RSI signals.

- This allows for capitalizing on trends while protecting profits and limiting losses.

4. **Risk-Reward Ratio:**

- Maintain a favorable risk-reward ratio. Ensure that potential profits justify the assumed risk in each trade.

Scenario-Based Risk Management:

1. **Trend Continuation:**

- If the trade is in the direction of the trend, consider trailing stops to capture potential extended moves.

- Regularly reassess RSI signals to confirm the trend's strength.

2. **Trend Reversal:**

- If the trade is based on a potential trend reversal signaled by RSI, set conservative profit targets and closely monitor for signs of the reversal losing momentum.

3. **Market Volatility:**

- In periods of heightened volatility, adjust position sizes and widen stop-loss levels to account for increased price fluctuations.

4. **News and Events:**

- Stay informed about scheduled economic events and news releases that may impact the market. Adjust risk management parameters accordingly.

Risk management is an ongoing process that requires adaptability to changing market conditions. By incorporating RSI signals into risk management strategies, traders can make informed decisions to protect their capital and optimize their risk-reward profiles. As we proceed, we will explore advanced RSI techniques and their applications in algorithmic trading and quantitative strategies.

CHAPTER 11

PSYCHOLOGICAL ASPECTS OF RSI TRADING

The psychological aspect of trading is a crucial determinant of success, and this holds true for RSI-based trading strategies. In this chapter, we will explore the impact of emotions and discipline in RSI trading, discuss common psychological challenges faced by traders, and provide insights into overcoming these challenges while maintaining a balanced mindset during market fluctuations.

Emotions and Discipline in RSI-Based Trading

1. **Impact of Emotions:**

   - Emotions, such as fear and greed, can significantly influence trading decisions. Emotional reactions to market movements may lead to impulsive actions, deviating from a well-thought-out RSI strategy.

2. **Discipline in Following Rules:**

   - Discipline is the ability to adhere to predefined trading rules, even in the face of emotional pressures. RSI-based strategies require discipline to execute trades based on objective signals rather than emotional reactions.

3. **Avoiding Overtrading:**

   - The excitement of potential profits or the desire to recover losses can lead to overtrading. Discipline involves sticking to a predefined trading plan and not deviating from it based on impulsive decisions.

Common Psychological Challenges and How to Overcome Them

1. **FOMO (Fear of Missing Out):**

   - **Challenge:** FOMO can lead to entering trades prematurely or chasing the market.

   - **Solution:** Remind yourself that missing one trade does not define success. Stick to the strategy and wait for favorable RSI signals.

2. **Loss Aversion:**

- **Challenge:** Traders may become overly concerned about avoiding losses, leading to prematurely closing winning trades or holding onto losing positions.

- **Solution:** Focus on the risk-reward ratio. Understand that losses are a natural part of trading and are manageable within a well-structured risk management plan.

3. **Impatience:**

   - **Challenge:** Impatience can lead to premature exits or entries, ignoring the importance of waiting for valid RSI signals.

   - **Solution:** Cultivate patience by understanding that quality trading opportunities may not present themselves every day. Waiting for clear signals is key to successful RSI trading.

4. **Confirmation Bias:**

   - **Challenge:** Traders may seek information that confirms their existing beliefs or biases, ignoring contradictory signals from RSI or other indicators.

   - **Solution:** Actively seek diverse perspectives and challenge your assumptions. Embrace a mindset of continuous learning and adaptation.

Maintaining a Balanced Mindset During Market Fluctuations

1. **Accepting Uncertainty:**

   - Acknowledge that markets are inherently uncertain, and not every trade will be a winner. Embrace uncertainty as an integral part of trading.

2. **Staying Calm in Drawdowns:**

   - During periods of drawdowns or losses, maintain emotional resilience. Stick to the trading plan and avoid making impulsive decisions driven by fear.

3. **Celebrating Successes:**

   - Acknowledge and celebrate successful trades. Positive reinforcement helps build confidence and reinforces discipline.

4. **Continuous Learning:**

   - Approach trading as an ongoing learning process. Each trade, whether a winner or a loser, provides valuable insights for improvement.

5. **Mindfulness Techniques:**

- Incorporate mindfulness techniques, such as deep breathing or meditation, to stay focused and calm during market fluctuations.

Developing a Psychological Edge:

1. **Self-Awareness:**

   - Develop self-awareness by regularly reflecting on your emotional responses to trading. Identify patterns and work on improving areas of weakness.

2. **Trading Journal:**

   - Maintain a trading journal to document trades, emotional reactions, and decisions. Analyzing past behavior can help identify and address psychological challenges.

3. **Mental Resilience:**

   - Cultivate mental resilience by embracing a long-term perspective. Individual trades are part of a larger journey, and setbacks are opportunities for growth.

4. **Professional Support:**

   - Consider seeking professional support, such as a trading coach or therapist, to work on psychological aspects and develop a resilient mindset.

Successfully navigating the psychological challenges of RSI trading involves ongoing self-reflection, discipline, and a commitment to continuous improvement. By addressing emotional reactions, maintaining discipline, and fostering a balanced mindset, traders can enhance their psychological resilience and increase their chances of long-term success. As we progress, we will explore advanced RSI techniques and their applications in algorithmic trading and quantitative strategies.

CHAPTER 12

CASE STUDIES

In this chapter, we will delve into detailed case studies to provide a practical understanding of successful RSI trades, learning from mistakes and losses, and showcasing real-world applications of RSI in diverse market scenarios.

Case Study 1: Successful RSI Trend-Following Trade

Market: Stock Market

Timeframe: Daily

Objective: Capture a trend in an individual stock.

Analysis:

- **Signal:** RSI consistently above 50, indicating a strong and sustained uptrend.

- **Confirmation:** Supported by the stock consistently trading above its 50-day Moving Average.

- **Entry:** Initiated a long position when RSI touched 40 during a brief pullback within the uptrend.

- **Exit:** Exited the trade when RSI reached 70, suggesting potential overextension. Profit realized during the sustained uptrend.

Lesson Learned:

- Successful trend-following with RSI requires patience and discipline.

- Combining RSI with Moving Averages can enhance trend confirmation.

Case Study 2: Learning from Mistakes

Market: Forex

Timeframe: 4-Hour

Objective: Identify and correct mistakes in a losing trade.

Analysis:

- **Signal:** Entered a short position based on RSI indicating overbought conditions.

- **Mistake:** Ignored bullish divergence forming on the 4-hour chart, indicating potential strength in the prevailing uptrend.

- **Loss:** The trade resulted in a significant loss as the currency pair continued its upward movement.

Lesson Learned:

- Always consider the broader context and potential divergences, even when RSI signals are strong.

- Admitting mistakes and learning from losses is crucial for continuous improvement.

Case Study 3: Real-World Applications in Cryptocurrency

Market: Cryptocurrency

Timeframe: 1-Hour

Objective: Identify potential reversals in a volatile cryptocurrency market.

Analysis:

- **Signal:** RSI formed bearish divergence with the price, indicating potential weakness in the uptrend.

- **Confirmation:** Supported by a key resistance level on the price chart.

- **Entry:** Short position initiated as RSI crossed below 70, confirming the potential reversal.

- **Exit:** Closed the position as RSI reached oversold levels, capturing a significant portion of the price correction.

Lesson Learned:

- Cryptocurrency markets can be highly responsive to RSI signals.

- Combining RSI with key support/resistance levels strengthens reversal signals.

Key Takeaways:

1. **Adaptability is Key:**

    - Each case study highlights the importance of adapting RSI strategies to different markets and timeframes.

2. **Confirmation is Crucial:**

    - Confirming RSI signals with other technical indicators or chart patterns enhances the reliability of trades.

3. **Continuous Learning:**

    - Learning from mistakes and losses is integral to evolving as a trader. A trading journal is a valuable tool for this purpose.

4. **Diverse Applications:**

- RSI is versatile and can be effectively applied across various markets, including stocks, forex, and cryptocurrencies.

5. **Risk Management Matters:**

- Case studies emphasize the role of risk management in protecting capital and mitigating losses.

By exploring these case studies, traders can gain insights into the practical application of RSI in different scenarios. Remember that no strategy is foolproof, and continuous learning and adaptation are essential for long-term success in trading. As we conclude this chapter, we will transition to advanced RSI techniques and explore their implementation in algorithmic trading and quantitative strategies.

CHAPTER 13

RSI AND MARKET SENTIMENT

Market sentiment plays a pivotal role in driving price movements, and the Relative Strength Index (RSI) can serve as a valuable tool for gauging and analyzing market sentiment. In this chapter, we will explore how RSI can be used to assess market sentiment, identify crowd behavior, and implement contrarian trading strategies based on sentiment analysis.

Gauging Market Sentiment with RSI

1. **Overbought and Oversold Conditions:**

   - RSI levels above 70 indicate overbought conditions, suggesting potential for a reversal or pullback.

- RSI levels below 30 signal oversold conditions, indicating potential buying opportunities.

2. **Extreme Readings as Sentiment Indicators:**

- Extreme RSI readings (near 0 or 100) may indicate strong sentiment in one direction. An RSI near 100 suggests strong buying pressure, while an RSI near 0 indicates strong selling pressure.

3. **Divergence Signals:**

- Divergence between RSI and price action can provide insight into changing sentiment. Bullish divergence in a downtrend may signal a shift in sentiment to the upside, and vice versa.

Using RSI to Identify Crowd Behavior

1. **Consensus Interpretation:**

- When RSI reaches extreme levels, it reflects a consensus among market participants. High RSI suggests widespread bullish sentiment, while low RSI indicates widespread bearish sentiment.

2. **Volume Confirmation:**

- Confirm RSI signals with volume analysis. Rising prices with increasing volume during overbought conditions may indicate strong bullish sentiment. Falling prices with increasing volume during oversold conditions may suggest strong bearish sentiment.

3. **Market Reaction to RSI Levels:**

- Observe how the market reacts to RSI levels. For example, if a stock consistently reverses when RSI reaches 70, it may indicate a prevailing sentiment among traders to sell at that level.

Contrarian Trading Strategies Based on RSI Sentiment Analysis

1. **Identifying Extremes for Reversals:**

- When RSI reaches extreme levels (above 70 or below 30), consider contrarian positions.

- Contrarian traders may sell when RSI is extremely high and buy when RSI is extremely low, anticipating a reversal in sentiment.

2. **Fade the Crowd:**

- Contrarian traders aim to "fade" the prevailing sentiment, meaning they go against the crowd.

- For example, if the majority is bullish and RSI is extremely high, contrarian traders might consider short positions.

3. **Confirming Sentiment Shifts:**

   - Use RSI divergence as a confirmation tool for contrarian trades.

   - If RSI shows bullish divergence in an overall bearish trend, it may signal a potential shift in sentiment, supporting a contrarian bullish trade.

Risk Management in Contrarian Trading:

1. **Tight Stop-Losses:**

   - Contrarian trades can be riskier, so employ tight stop-loss orders to manage risk effectively.

2. **Confirmation from Other Indicators:**

   - Confirm RSI-based contrarian signals with other technical indicators or price action to enhance reliability.

3. **Gradual Position Building:**

   - Consider building contrarian positions gradually rather than entering a full position at once. This allows for adjustments based on evolving market conditions.

Real-World Considerations:

1. **News and Events:**

- Be aware of upcoming news and events that could influence sentiment independently of technical indicators.

2. **Market Conditions:**

   - Assess the overall market conditions. Contrarian strategies may be more effective in ranging or sideways markets than in strong trends.

3. **Long-Term Sentiment Trends:**

   - Consider the long-term sentiment trend. Contrarian trades against a prevailing long-term sentiment may be riskier than those aligning with it.

By incorporating RSI into sentiment analysis, traders can gain valuable insights into the prevailing market sentiment and use contrarian strategies to capitalize on sentiment shifts. However, it's essential to approach contrarian trading with caution and employ robust risk management practices. As we progress, we will explore advanced RSI techniques and their applications in algorithmic trading and quantitative strategies.

CHAPTER 14

RSI AND FUNDAMENTAL ANALYSIS

In this chapter, we will explore the integration of the Relative Strength Index (RSI) with fundamental analysis, highlighting the synergy between technical and fundamental factors. Additionally, we will discuss RSI's role in identifying potential market-moving events and how traders can benefit from a holistic approach that combines both technical and fundamental perspectives.

Integrating RSI with Fundamental Factors

1. **Understanding Fundamental Analysis:**

    - Fundamental analysis involves evaluating the intrinsic value of an asset based on economic, financial, and qualitative factors.

- Key elements include earnings reports, economic indicators, company financials, and geopolitical events.

2. **Combining RSI with Fundamental Indicators:**

   - Integrate RSI signals with fundamental factors to enhance trading decisions.

   - For example, consider taking a long position based on RSI signals when supported by positive earnings reports or economic data.

3. **Economic Calendar and RSI:**

   - Use an economic calendar to align RSI trades with scheduled economic releases.

   - For instance, refrain from entering trades just before major economic announcements to avoid unexpected volatility.

Finding the Synergy between Technical and Fundamental Analysis

1. **Confirming Technical Signals with Fundamentals:**

   - Confirm RSI signals with fundamental factors to increase confidence in trade decisions.

   - A bullish RSI signal accompanied by positive earnings growth or favorable economic conditions may strengthen the trade rationale.

2. **Aligning Long-Term Trends:**

   - Consider the long-term fundamental trends when analyzing the overall market direction.

   - If RSI signals align with the prevailing fundamental trends, it may provide a stronger basis for trade decisions.

3. **Market Sentiment and Economic Factors:**

   - Evaluate RSI as a gauge of market sentiment and align it with broader economic factors.

   - If RSI indicates a strong bullish sentiment and economic indicators support positive market conditions, it may reinforce the decision to enter a long position.

RSI's Role in Identifying Potential Market-Moving Events

1. **Volatility Around Events:**

   - Certain fundamental events, such as earnings releases or economic reports, can trigger increased market volatility.

   - RSI can help identify potential overbought or oversold conditions around these events.

2. **Anticipating Reactions to News:**

- RSI signals may help anticipate market reactions to news or events.

- For example, if RSI is in overbought territory ahead of an earnings release, it may indicate that positive expectations are already priced in.

3. **Risk Management in Event-Driven Trading:**

- Use RSI to assess risk around event-driven trading.

- Tighten stop-loss levels or reduce position sizes when RSI signals extreme conditions, indicating potential for sharp and unpredictable price movements.

Real-World Considerations:

1. **Earnings Season and RSI:**

- During earnings season, consider how RSI aligns with expectations and actual results to refine trading strategies.

2. **Central Bank Announcements:**

- Central bank announcements can have a significant impact on currency markets. RSI signals can help gauge potential reactions.

3. **Geopolitical Events:**

- Be mindful of geopolitical events and align RSI signals with potential market responses to geopolitical developments.

4. **Macro-Economic Trends:**

   - Consider the broader economic trends when analyzing RSI signals. A bullish RSI signal may carry more weight in an environment of overall economic growth.

Conclusion:

By integrating RSI with fundamental analysis, traders can create a more comprehensive and well-rounded approach to decision-making. This synergy enables traders to leverage both technical and fundamental factors, providing a more nuanced understanding of market dynamics. As we progress, we will delve into advanced RSI techniques and explore their applications in algorithmic trading and quantitative

CHAPTER 15

ADVANCED RSI TECHNIQUES

In this chapter, we will delve into advanced concepts and techniques related to the Relative Strength Index (RSI). As technology continues to evolve, we will explore how machine learning and artificial intelligence can be incorporated with RSI, and we'll highlight cutting-edge applications that keep traders at the forefront of innovation.

Exploring Advanced RSI Concepts and Techniques

1. **Adaptive RSI Periods:**

   - Rather than using fixed periods, explore adaptive RSI periods that adjust based on market conditions.

- Adaptive RSI adapts to volatility, potentially providing more accurate signals in dynamic markets.

2. **Smoothed RSI:**

   - Apply smoothing techniques to RSI, such as using exponential moving averages (EMAs) on RSI values.

   - Smoothed RSI can help filter out noise and provide a clearer view of the underlying trend.

3. **RSI Divergence Confirmation:**

   - Confirm RSI divergence signals with additional technical indicators or chart patterns.

   - For instance, combine RSI divergence with MACD or price action patterns to strengthen reversal signals.

4. **Volume-Weighted RSI:**

   - Incorporate volume information into RSI calculations.

   - Volume-weighted RSI gives more weight to periods with higher trading volume, providing a nuanced view of market strength or weakness.

Incorporating Machine Learning and Artificial Intelligence with RSI

1. **Predictive RSI Models:**

   - Develop predictive models using machine learning algorithms to forecast RSI movements.

   - Historical price data, volume, and additional technical indicators can be input features for training machine learning models.

2. **Algorithmic Trading with RSI:**

   - Implement algorithmic trading strategies that dynamically adjust based on RSI signals.

   - Machine learning algorithms can optimize trading parameters in real-time, adapting to changing market conditions.

3. **Sentiment Analysis:**

   - Integrate natural language processing (NLP) algorithms to analyze market sentiment from news articles, social media, or financial reports.

   - Combine sentiment analysis with RSI to gauge market sentiment and make more informed trading decisions.

Staying Ahead with Cutting-Edge RSI Applications

1. **Quantitative Strategies:**

- Explore quantitative strategies that leverage RSI as a component in a broader algorithmic trading framework.

- Quantitative models can adapt to various market conditions and exploit inefficiencies.

2. **High-Frequency Trading (HFT) Strategies:**

- Develop high-frequency trading strategies that capitalize on rapid price movements based on RSI signals.

- HFT algorithms can execute trades in milliseconds, leveraging RSI for quick decision-making.

3. **Dynamic Portfolio Optimization:**

- Use RSI as part of a dynamic portfolio optimization strategy.

- Machine learning algorithms can continuously adjust portfolio weights based on RSI signals, optimizing returns and managing risk.

4. **Intermarket Analysis with RSI:**

- Apply RSI to intermarket analysis by considering correlations between different asset classes.

- Machine learning algorithms can identify patterns and relationships between RSI signals in various markets.

Risk Management in Advanced RSI Applications:

1. **Machine Learning Validation:**

   - Validate machine learning models with rigorous testing and backtesting procedures.

   - Ensure that the models generalize well to unseen market conditions.

2. **Dynamic Risk Controls:**

   - Implement dynamic risk controls that adapt to the evolving parameters of advanced RSI applications.

   - Machine learning algorithms can adjust risk parameters based on changing market dynamics.

3. **Continuous Monitoring:**

   - Continuously monitor and reassess the performance of advanced RSI applications.

   - Rapid technological advancements require ongoing evaluation to stay ahead of potential challenges or model decay.

Conclusion:

As technology advances, traders can leverage advanced RSI techniques to gain a competitive edge in the market. Incorporating machine learning, artificial intelligence, and cutting-edge applications with RSI allows for more sophisticated analyses and adaptive trading strategies. However, it's crucial to approach these advanced techniques with a thorough understanding of their limitations and risks, and to continuously monitor and optimize their performance in dynamic market conditions. With these tools, traders can explore new frontiers in the world of quantitative and algorithmic trading.